MIRACLES IN THE GARDEN

"Building a Butterfly Garden and Raising Monarch Butterflies"

LAURA M DURAND ELKINS

Scripture taken from the King James Version of the Bible.

WestBow Press books may be ordered through booksellers or by contacting:

WestBow Press
A Division of Thomas Nelson & Zondervan
1663 Liberty Drive
Bloomington, IN 47403
www.westbowpress.com
1 (866) 928-1240

ISBN: 978-1-9736-6018-7 (sc)
ISBN: 978-1-9736-6019-4 (e)

Library of Congress Control Number: 2019904407

Print information available on the last page.

WestBow Press rev. date: 04/24/2019

WESTBOW PRESS®
A DIVISION OF THOMAS NELSON & ZONDERVAN

MIRACLES IN THE GARDEN

"Building A Butterfly Garden And
Raising Monarch Butterflies"

Told by Laura M Durand Elkins
Lancaster, Texas

Biography

Laura Marie Durand Elkins
Lives in Lancaster, Texas
Retired EMT-Paramedic II
Owner of "The Medic Gardener"
I raise and release Monarch and Queen Butterflies.

Acknowledgements

Thank you to my wonderful and supportive husband Scott. You have helped me more than you will ever know. I love you.

Thank you to Paul H. for your awesome help on clearing out the ground and making this beautiful garden possible. You're the best.

Thank you to Aaron D. for helping with the clearing out, the ground prep, and the planting of the beautiful plants in the garden. This project would not have been possible without your wonderful help. You are amazing.

Thank you to Will S. for the use of your microscope. I would have never known the amazing detail that the hand of God created without the use of this amazing device. Taking the photos and sharing them to this book was my greatest joy. You were instrumental in opening my eyes to God's handiwork. Thank you my friend.

Thank you to Nathan E. for designing the front cover of this book. You have an amazing gift and I really appreciate you for sharing that with me on this venture.

Authors Note

Our God, the Sovereign and masterful creator of all living things both complex and beautiful did one of His most incredible creations when He designed the Monarch butterfly. Not only is this creation complex and beautiful but it also an insect that can only be explained by intelligent design due to its extraordinary life.

I love this particular butterfly because it not only brings attention to an amazing creator, but it has also baffled evolutionary scientists by what the Monarch does. The Monarch butterfly is the only long distance migrating insect. With perfection and remarkable precision that has never been figured out by scientist, the Monarch travels approximately 3000 miles against all odds from the northern US and Nova Scotia, Canada all the way down to the Michoacan Forest in Mexico to the Monarch Butterfly Biosphere Reserve. There are now Monarchs that stay year round from central Florida south and the Monarchs on the West Coast that migrate to the Pacific Grove in southern California. Not all migrate to Mexico.

The Monarch Butterfly goes through four stages of development before it becomes a butterfly. No one knows why it takes four stages of life, all we know is that it happens according to God's will, purposes and good pleasure. I believe His purpose for this magnificent creation was to show the evolutionary that this indeed can only be explained by an intelligent Creator who is Yahweh.

I raise Monarchs at my home from a Butterfly Garden I had built. While a female Monarch will lay approximately 250 to 500 eggs, only 10% will make it to becoming a butterfly due to all the predators.

It is because of these great odds that I decided to find as many Monarch eggs as possible and raise them indoors.

I have always loved the outdoors. Gardening along with butterfly and bird watching has always been a big part of my love for being outdoors. It never ceases to amaze me the wonderful and detailed work of God in the beauty of flowers and the wonderful pollinator's and visitors that the flowers attract. The year 2018 was my first year to focus on butterflies and their host plants. The monarch and queen butterfly in particular sparked my great interest. These two butterflies as caterpillars are the only ones that feed on the milkweed plant leaves while in this stage. At the time I also noticed several circulating articles saying that the monarch's numbers had been declining in the past 10 years and that a nationwide effort was out to help raise the numbers back up by building pesticide-free butterfly habitats in gardens. I instantly wanted to be a part of this effort. It is with heavy heart to mention that the farmers' use of pesticides and the homeowners' use of weed-resistant material and herbicides are the main reason for the declining numbers of the Monarch. The common milkweed plant grows naturally in a lot of open grasslands here in the southern part of Dallas, Texas where there are several open farmlands and plains. Because of this, the monarchs and queens are everywhere in heavy numbers from late July to mid-October and it's an incredible sight to see. Who wouldn't want to be part of this great effort?

I am happy to say that by the end of the season, I ended up home raising and releasing over 55 monarchs and 59 queens. Nothing brought me more pleasure than this.

Years ago, my mother, Lucy A. Scholz, planted the seed in me for the love of flowers, and I also wanted to build a butterfly and bird garden in her memory. We moved from Minneapolis, MN to Farmers Branch, Texas in 1969. It was at this home where I saw my mother explode with happiness because she finally made it to the South where she could garden till her hearts content. My mother's love for flowers always fascinated me. I never saw her more at peace and happier than when she was looking at, receiving, or planting flowers around the house. When I was a young girl I remember on several occasions picking simple flowering weeds on the way home from school to give them to my mother. She always had the biggest smile ever! Flowers brought happiness to my mom, and just the idea of putting in this garden has come with much joy and happiness of those great memories.

This book will be the beginning of a series of books that will cover the different visitors to the garden, including other butterflies and birds that visit or live in the garden. These fun stories will be about individual and named Butterflies and Birds that were either in-home raised and studied or studied in their natural habitat. I promise you will be entertained while learning about these absolutely beautiful creations God has ever designed. Writing this book has brought me many smiles and I hope it does the same to those special people who read it.

"It's springtime! Let's Go."

Don't you just love butterflies? Let's take on a project and build a butterfly and hummingbird garden in the back yard. I'm going to need some help. How would you like to help me out? It's won't be easy, but it will sure pay off when we're done. "Great, let's get started."

We have to start by mapping out the area that we want our garden to go. Then, we have to get our good friend, Paul, to come over and help us out. He brought his tractor over and is going to dig out all the old grass, rocks, and debris. It will make the soil loose for planting our new butterfly and hummingbird plants. We sure thank Paul for helping us out.

Aaron, one of the best gardeners I know, has come to help me plant the flowers in the garden now that the area is prepped and ready for planting. Aaron first tilled (mixed in) nutrients in the soil and then he put down cardboard and wet it real good before planting. The cardboard helps to keep the weeds out. Once the plants are planted, two inches of mulch will go over the cardboard and around all the plants. This will help keep the dirt moist underneath during those hot Texas summer days. The garden will look so good when it's completed.

"Look how nicely it turned out." Several Butterfly friendly plants are in the garden now. We planted a lot of yellow and red Tropical Milkweed, because this the host plant for the Monarch and Queen Butterfly caterpillars. We also planted Lantana's, Durante's, Turks Cap, Butterfly bushes, Firecrackers, Pentas, Verbena's, Echinacea, Zinnias, Black-eyed Susans, Indian Paint Brush, Foxglove, and a few others. I need to mention that the Hummingbirds love these plants as well. I placed a colorful bottle tree in the garden too to add some fun. It is now time to wait a month or two for the plants to mature. It is very important to water the garden every day during those two months to make sure the roots grow and become strong and healthy.

It has been a couple of months now and the plants have all matured and are in full bloom. We just have to wait and see what comes to the garden. "Look, I see two monarchs and two queen butterflies on the tropical milkweed. Don't they look a lot alike?" What can you see that is different about the two? Let's go look for eggs on the back of the leaves. The eggs of a monarch and the eggs of the queen look exactly alike. We need to watch the monarch closely to make sure we see where she lays her eggs. The monarch eggs have less than a 10% chance of survival in the wild due to predator bugs so we are going to collect monarch eggs. A female will lay approximately 500 eggs in her lifetime, so we have to do what we can to help their chances.

"Look at all the eggs we found." We just saved four monarchs from being hunted by wasps, fire ants, the milkweed bug, and spiders to name a few. We brought them inside and plan on raising them till they become beautiful monarch butterflies. We now have to very lightly dip them in water for 60 seconds to wash off any disease that might have been left on them by predators. "Don't you feel good about rescuing these eggs?" Before we prepare these for protection, let's take a look at the eggs under a microscope.

"Look at the amazing detail of the egg under the microscope."

As you can see from the egg on my finger, it is the size of a pencil tip. While we are talking about the egg, let's talk about the life cycle of the monarch butterfly. There are four stages of transformation. The first stage is the egg, the second stage is the larvae (caterpillar), the third stage is the pupa (chrysalis), and the fourth stage emerges as an adult butterfly. The monarch also has four generations that are all different butterflies from that generation series. The first through third generation Monarchs only live six to eight weeks. The fourth and final monarch (the migration one) is the generation that will live six to eight months. It will migrate south for the winter, hibernate, mate, and then head back north in the spring to lay eggs. The new generation starts all over again in the spring when the eggs hatch.

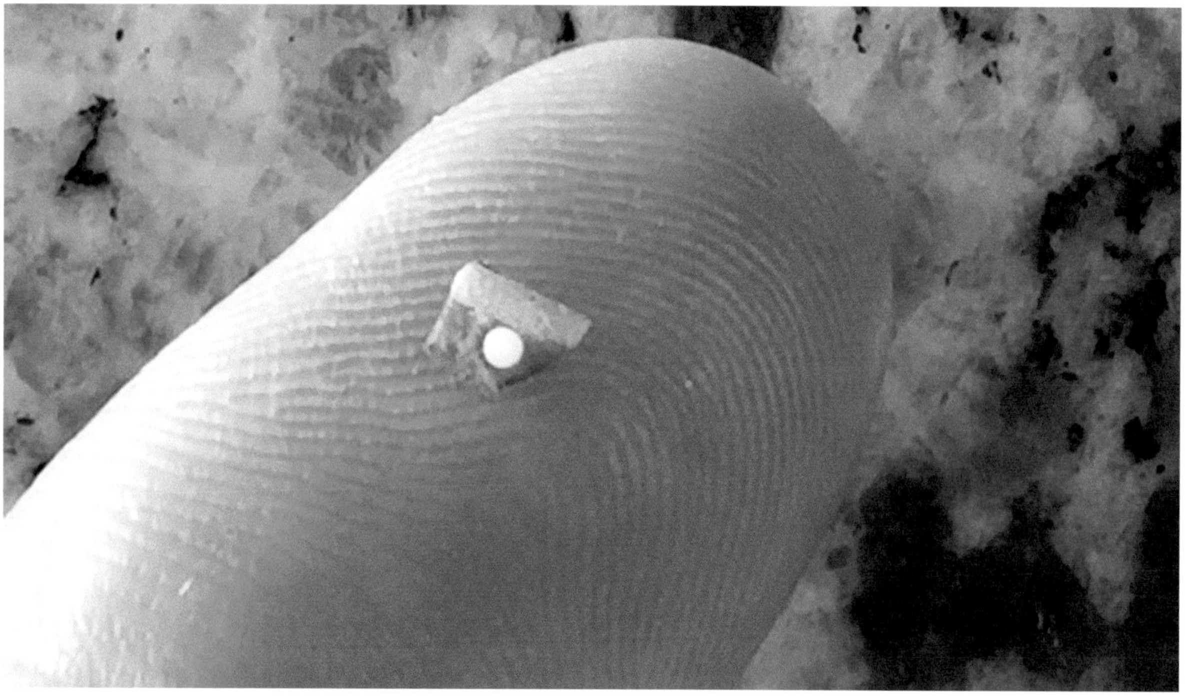

"Ok, time to protect these eggs." We don't want to disturb them by touching with human hands yet, so we need to cut out a tiny piece of the milkweed leaf with the egg on it, and place it on a paper towel and lay them in a vented container.

Make sure you keep the container away from direct sunlight as it will create too much moisture build up in the container and bad bacteria could set in and cause harm to the eggs. We must now wait three to four days for them to hatch.

After four days, we'll put one of the eggs under the microscope and see if the caterpillar is ready to come out.

Just before it is ready, the tip of the egg will be black. That is his head, and that is where he will start eating his way out of the shell. The caterpillar will eat its shell when it emerges. This will be the first meal of its life. "Oh, look! The little guy has hatched from his shell. Isn't he just the cutest little thing?" He just started the Instar stage 1.

Look at the tiny pair of tentacles right behind his head and another pair by his tail end. This is how you know it's a monarch caterpillar. A queen butterfly caterpillar looks like the monarch caterpillar except the queen has three pair of tentacles.

"Look how small it looks on my finger." This is a few hours after hatching. Notice that this caterpillar has three pair of tentacles. See one pair behind his head, in the middle of the body, and the tail end. This is a Queen caterpillar. See how similar they look?

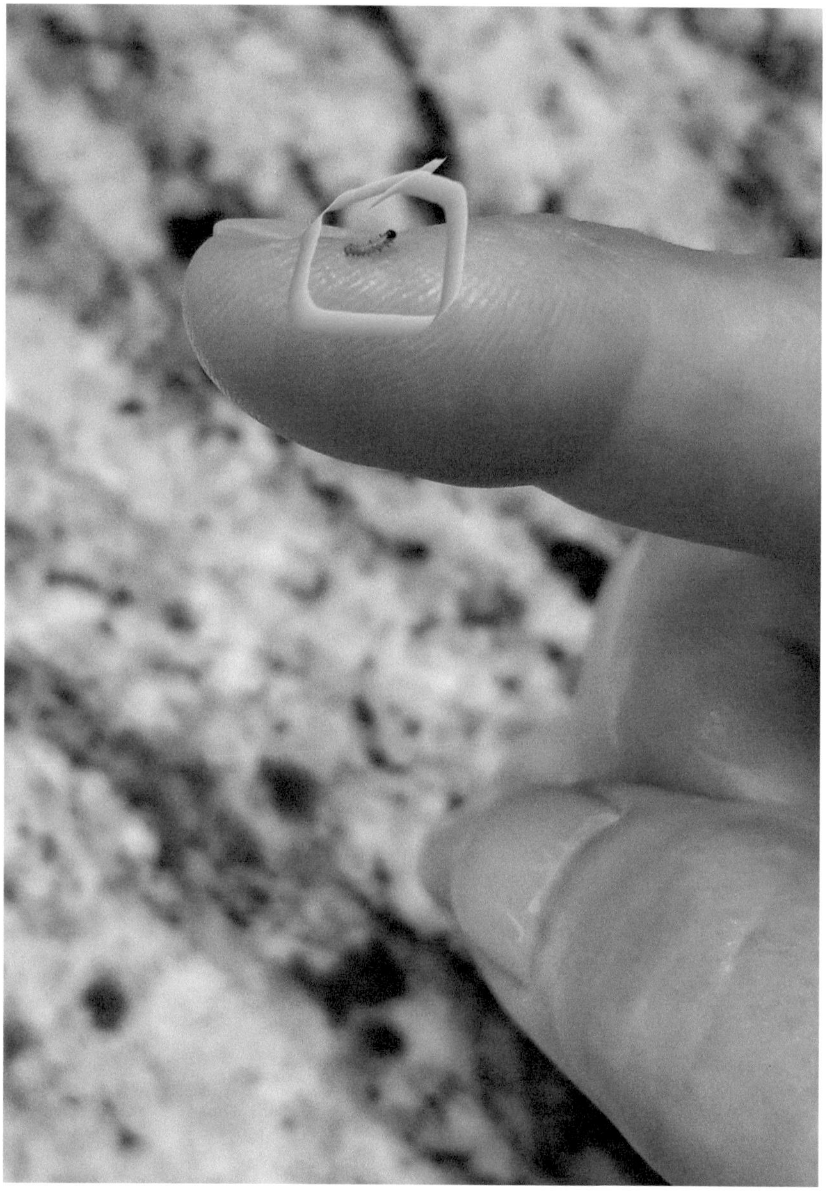

It is time to put the new caterpillars on fresh new leaves so they can continue to grow. The monarch caterpillar can only eat milkweed leaves. White milky sap within the milkweed plant contains a chemical called cardenolides that is poisonous. The fluid within the plant allows the caterpillar to defend itself from being attacked or eaten. The milkweed toxin remains in the monarch and queen butterfly throughout the complete life cycle.

Let me tell you about the five Instar stages of the monarch caterpillar. They grow and shed their skin and head capsule during these stages. They must not be disturbed or touched as there new skin will be wet. The skin needs time to dry out and harden into a new, silky layer. You will be able to measure the caterpillars as a way of determining what Instar stage they are in: Instar stage 1 (2-6mm), Instar stage 2 (6-9mm), Instar stage 3 (10-14mm), Instar stage 4 (13-25mm), Instar stage 5 (25-45mm). For reference: ½″ = 12.7mm

It has been a couple of days, time to move them to another leaf. We do this by cutting a small square on the leaf they are currently on and move that piece to a new leaf. You have to transfer them to new leaves like this for a few days because they are too small and delicate for human hands to handle.

Can anyone tell me the Instar stage of the monarch caterpillar located in the picture? That's right! It is in Instar stage 5. This one is actually 5mm bigger than the stage 5 numbers at 50mm. She will be a big beautiful monarch.

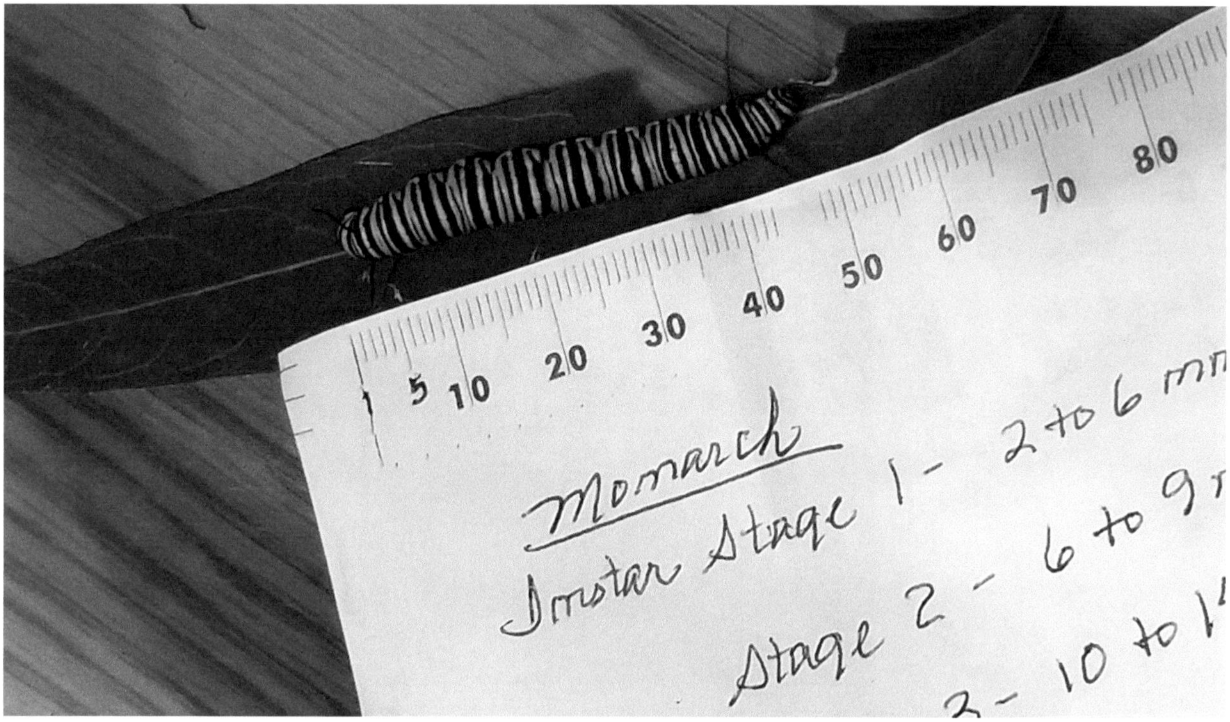

It has been a few days now and we have been changing out the milkweed leaves and cleaning the containers from the green frass (caterpillar droppings) every day. It is very important to keep the containers clean due to bacteria in the frass that can cause harm to the caterpillars. Let's go to the next page and see how big they have grown.

The caterpillars just shed their layer of skin and head capsule. They are 11mm long now. The caterpillars are now at Instar stage 3. This is what there shedding skin and head capsule look like under a microscope. Isn't it cool? Look how big they are getting. At this stage the monarch caterpillar is starting to eat more leaves in a day. You have to make sure you have plenty of milkweed leaves to feed all the caterpillars you raise. Luckily for us, we planted plenty of tropical milkweed plants.

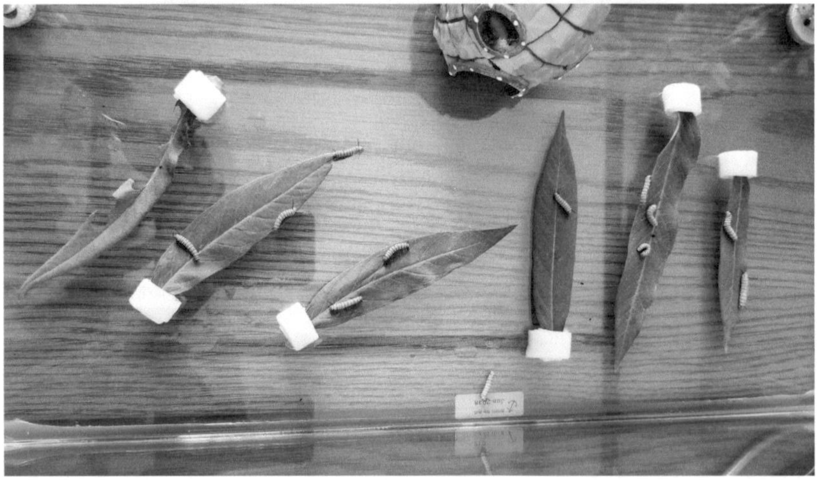

We are having a nice warm summer so far and we have some guests that have joined us on the milkweed plants. Meet the tiny yellow aphids. They like to suck the sap on the back of the milkweed leaf and can be damaging to the plant over time. They don't bother the caterpillars but they are a nuisance to them. All I can say is, thank goodness for lady bugs. It is the lady bug that feed on the aphids and keeps their numbers under control. I see another guest; this is the milkweed bug. This bug is red and black and can be seen in two sizes and with slightly different patterns on their backs. This bug likes to feed on the seeds of the milkweed plant. We have to brush them off occasionally to keep the plant healthy.

It's been a couple more days, so let's check on the caterpillars. "Wow, look how big they are getting." They just shed there last skin layer and made it to Instar stage 5. This is a very important stage because the more milkweed leaves they consume, the bigger and healthier they will be. All the leaves they are consuming in this stage will be the main fuel that gets them through the ten to twelve days of being in chrysalis and the first three days as an adult butterfly.

The monarch caterpillar has three distinct body parts: a head, thorax and abdomen. The head has a pair of very short tentacles, their mouth consist of an upper lip, mandibles (jaw), a lower lip, and a spinneret (web spinner). They have six pairs of very simple eyes, called ocelli. Even with all of these eyes, the caterpillar's vision is very poor; they can only see light and dark.

Our monarch caterpillars are now going through a leaf an hour. This is the stage they eat the most. I love stage 5 because the caterpillar is soft to the touch and they are so active. It's fun to feed them by hand, they are so cute.

I'll bet you would like to see what their feet look like. They are like little suckers and they stick to everything. Can you count the number of feet that are gripping the milkweed leaf stem?

They have three pair of front jointed legs, and five pair of false legs (prolegs) that follow the length of the abdomen. Do you see his tentacles? They function as his sense organ. They use the tentacles more because their eye site is poor.

The Instar stage 5 caterpillars have been eating non-stop for two days and have consumed many, many leaves. Any time now, the caterpillars will have eaten all they can in order to prepare themselves for a climb up to a place where they can J-Hang. The J-Hang is when the monarch caterpillar has to find a safe place to spin a tight platform of webbing so it can hang upside down in the shape of a "J". During this period of about 12 to 16 hours, the caterpillar is preparing its body to transform into what is called a chrysalis.

The monarch caterpillar has now hung in the J-Hang for about thirteen hours, and it is wiggling around a bit getting ready to shed its skin and become a chrysalis. This process normally takes about 10 minutes, until the last wiggle and the final skin layer drops from the chrysalis. Continuous changes actually occur during the caterpillar stage. The wings and other adult organs develop from tiny clusters of cells already present in the caterpillar, and by the time it goes into chrysalis, the major changes to the adult butterfly have already begun.

During the chrysalis stage this transformation is completed. Notice the color of the chrysalis as it finishes its transformation. It is light green with yellow markings. At this stage, it is very soft. When it finishes, it turns a jade green and becomes a hard protective shell. It takes about 12 hours to completely harden.

The chrysalis has been in this state for about 10 days. When you see that the chrysalis becomes transparent and you can see the monarch wing color, know that the beautiful butterfly is just minutes away from emerging. Once the transparent chrysalis starts cracking, the whole process takes approximately fifteen to twenty seconds for the monarch butterfly to emerge. Once it arrives, the wings will be wrinkled for approximately fifteen minutes.

When the monarch finally stretches out its wings, they will be wet and need to dry for two hours before they are ready to fly off or be released. You will know when they are ready to fly off because they will be flapping their wings slowly and start moving about. We had several monarchs emerge within minutes of each other; it was so exciting.

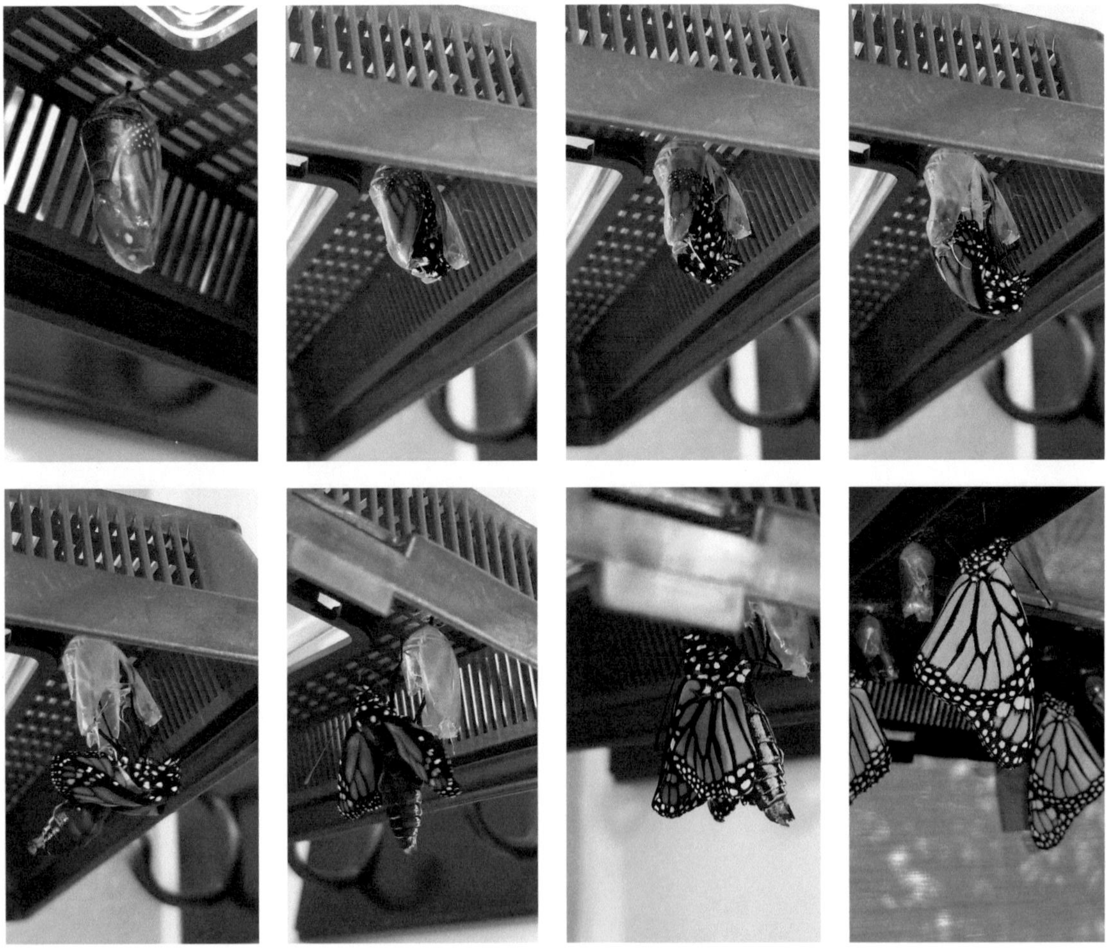

"Didn't it feel great to raise our first few Monarchs and set them free? All of you were a great help and should feel very proud."

Once we release the first generation monarch, it will stay around in the garden for a few days in order to get its bearings before it continues on its northward journey for the summer. In late August, early September, we will have another big batch of Monarch eggs to collect. This will be the fourth generation that will head south to Michoacan, Mexico on the great migration. The monarchs will stay six to eight months to hibernate, mate and return to lay eggs next spring.

Here is a male and female monarch we raised and released in the garden, two of many that were released. What do you see different between the male and female monarch? That's right! The male has two "dots" on his lower wings. Those are his scent glands that he uses to attract a female.

There were several other butterflies that visited the garden throughout the season. I look forward to raising the queen butterfly with all my helpers in the next book. Thank you for going on this wonderful journey with me, you all are awesome.

The End of the Beginning

"All things were made through Him, and without Him was not anything made that was made."
John 1:3 (KJV)

If you are interested in more information about monarchs and other butterflies along with more information on building a butterfly garden, here are some other wonderful resources that helped me out tremendously in this venture.

"The Life Cycles of Butterflies"
By Judy & Wayne Richards

"Monarchs and Milkweed"
By Anuray Agrawal

"Gardening for Butterflies"
By The Xerces Society

"Lone Star Gardening"
By Neil Sperry

Websites: monarchwatch.com, monarch-butterfly.com,
monarchbutterflyusa.com, butterflywebsite.com
Oakleaf Landscape & Tree Service (www.oakleaftree.com)
Texas Discovery Gardens (www.txdg.org)

Printed in the United States
By Bookmasters